P9-DVC-791

DAYS OF AWE

DAYS OF AWE

POEMS BY MAURYA SIMON

COPPER CANYON PRESS

THE PUBLICATION OF THIS BOOK WAS SUPPORTED
BY A GRANT FROM THE NATIONAL ENDOWMENT
FOR THE ARTS

COPPER CANYON PRESS IS IN RESIDENCE WITH CENTRUM
AT FORT WORDEN STATE PARK

ISBN : 1-55659-023-7
LIBRARY OF CONGRESS CATALOG CARD NUMBER: 88-63224
COPYRIGHT © 1989 BY MAURYA SIMON
ALL RIGHTS RESERVED

THE TYPE IS GALLIARD, DESIGNED BY MATTHEW CARTER
TYPE SET BY THE TYPEWORKS, VANCOUVER, B.C.
BOOK DESIGNED BY TREE SWENSON

COVER BY BAILA GOLDENTHAL
"GOLD LEAF SERIES #3"

COPPER CANYON PRESS
POST OFFICE BOX 271
PORT TOWNSEND
WASHINGTON 98368

The author wishes to thank the editors of the following magazines in which these poems originally appeared:

ARETE: *Clothes that Wear Me*
BLACK WARRIOR REVIEW: *Vermeer's Women*
CUMBERLAND POETRY REVIEW: *Contusion, King Midas's Daughter*
THE ELEPHANT-EAR: *At Seventeen*
THE GEORGIA REVIEW: *The Poem at the End of the World, The Future*
THE HUDSON REVIEW: *Boy Crazy*
IRONWOOD: *Tale before the End of the World*
THE LITERARY REVIEW: *Angle of Repose*
THE LITTLE MAGAZINE: *Nude Mice*
MICHIGAN QUARTERLY REVIEW: *At Mudumalai*
THE MISSOURI REVIEW: *In the Shtetl*
MOSAIC: *Death's Earned No Diplomas*
MSS.: *Atomic Psalm*
ONTARIO REVIEW: *The Abandoned Church*
PANOPLY: *The Gardener*
PASSAGES NORTH: *The Years*
POETRY: *The Sadness of Rivers, Theme and Variations*
POETRY EAST: *Dream Babies, Madras Lament*
RACCOON: *The Pharaohs*
THE REAPER: *Commander-in-Chief Road, The White Cockroach*
ROANOKE REVIEW: *The Rabbi's Trousers, Circa 1900*
SALMAGUNDI: *The Palmist, The Surreal Man*
THE SEATTLE REVIEW: *For Naomi*
SENECA REVIEW: *In the Valley of Ether*
THE SOUTHERN REVIEW: *Breakwater*
TRIQUARTERLY: *Les Fleurs du Printemps, Rothko's Black*
VERSE: *Icarus in the Twentieth Century*
WEST BRANCH: *Survival*
WILLOW SPRINGS: *Sunday, Encounter*

"The Sadness of Rivers" was reprinted in the *1988 Anthology of Magazine Verse and Yearbook of American Poetry.*

I am indebted to Sam Hamill and Tree Swenson for their unfailing good taste and artistic support, and to Richard Tillinghast, my first mentor and friend of many years.

For my sister Tamara

TABLE OF CONTENTS

I

II

III

I AM FILLED WITH LOVE

AS A GREAT TREE WITH WIND,

AS A SPONGE WITH THE OCEAN,

AS A GREAT LIFE WITH SUFFERING,

AS TIME WITH DEATH.

—Anna Swir

I

Dedication

If ever I had a muse, it was you,
your artist's hands narrow and white,
your eyes so amazingly blue

they seem to overtake the world
and re-tinge it; your familiar face
always hovering in and out of mine.

A certain violence in likenesses,
and in our differences, makes
you my most solid witness –

and at times you're the only door
my being passes through, as if
through a curtain made of flesh

that parts us each in two, splitting
us into yin and yang, those forces
eternally at odds, and at one.

There are things to say that we
have never said, and are likely
to forget or softly put away

along with the old arguments,
the jealousies and dreads.
But let me say, if anything,

that you're my telltale tongue,
my luminous eye, my fountain pen.
I owe you everything that's good

upon the page, and even my rage
over what's bad, false, leaden.
If I can claim but one truth won,

it's that you gave me first what
I didn't have: another self to love
unconditionally, and to forgive.

Sunday

We carry the long mirrors of the afternoon,
each from our separate windows.
Paper men and women, we waver
as a breeze lifts the curtains and ruffles
our vision. The city, bitten by cold
and drowned in fog, rises to meet us.
How far away we are from our own lives;
they float beyond us like the cries
of gulls circling the docks.
What are our lives but gestures
from God's left hand, or else a shuddering
that sleep can neither cure nor quiet?

Down in the street, a woman rests her back
against a windowpane, a businessman in black
resets his watch, a dog barks at a bus.
All the hungers dressed in living flesh,
all the half-lit shadows, burning blood,
the irresistable stories, days of incense.
For each word, ten thousand movements.

Tell me, spirits of the Bay, spirits
of the pestle pounding out more spirits,
is every corner peopled by blind prophets?
All we can do is try to assemble the little hums
of our lives in utter darkness.
Thought linked to act, we try and try.
We stretch and burrow, row and sprint,
then awaken drenched in pools of sadness.

A host of angels, in the guise of acorns,
falls, and northward towards Canada,

the geese return, holding in their beaks
long, skinny straws of rain.
The breath of our ancestors is upon us.
Their grief overhangs the earth,
their joy borrows our bodies in puffs of air.
To say I love is to live; to say
I love is to tumble head over heels
into the arms of light.

Breakwater

Under the huge, oily, half-barnacled rocks,
my sister and I fished every Saturday for crabs.
We lived to see them foam wildly at the mouth,
their curved claws clacking like pinking shears
against the fabric of their fear, their nubby eyes
black-stemmed and blind, searching for ours.
We hated and loved them zealously, as we did
the sand sharks who wore grim faces on their backs;
the jellyfish, with their colonies of purple barbs;
the helpless grunion dying in phosphorescent glory;
the riptides that, over the years, carried us
miles from shore. All the dangers of the ocean
called to us back then, just as our mother called
out our sweet names, so as to spell us into being.
It was danger we thought we longed for,
more than love; for love seemed always dry-
docked, a dead-end, whereas the sea-slung wind
was heavy with mystery as it swept in whiffs
of pirate ships, bloodied rags, sirens, and tar.
Those nights we slipped out my sister's window,
climbed down the wooden siding of the second floor,
alighted on bicycles, flew off in our nightgowns
down the empty esplanade to King Harbor;
those nights we climbed the breakwater, leaping
like ghosts in darkness from rock to rock,
as waves boiled over our toes: we had to hold on
to each other's waist to keep from diving in.
Leap, leap the spindrift spat out at us,

the thrumming swells undulating their bellies
over the closed womb of the blackened water.
Something in the fast-moving clouds overhead
made us listen to our own breathing; something
vast and ageless, like an old grief, ever singing
its salt in our veins: the ocean calling us home.

Boy Crazy

I used to watch the roses loosen
their pink wigs as I clocked the rain.
One-two, one-two, the drops plunked
the petals down into the gutter.
Drenched, I strolled my way into town
hoping to meet the boy I shuddered
to think of, the boy with hair black
as patent leather, the boy with the sneer
that dangled like a cigaret from his lips.
I was feverish with innocence, my skin
aglow, my shadow almost voluptuous.
Past the blue houses and an old Volvo
backfiring from an alley, past
The Lighthouse where once Dizzy Gillespie
had blown me a kiss when I was twelve,
past the Mermaid Restaurant where I first
saw my father flirt with a fierce waitress,
I finally made my way to the pier.
Only one fisherman crouched near a pail
of squid, and his hair was yellow.
The sound of rain was swallowed by waves
pounding the shore with white fists.
Over Catalina half a rainbow perched
like a tweezed eyebrow raised in surprise.
I kept track of how late he was,
while clouds paired up on the horizon,
and the minutes fell away like bits
of torn paper into the surf. But,
he came, after all. Dizzy, elated,
faint with restraint, I played it cool.
Kiss me, kiss me, he whispered, sneering
his powerful sneer as he bent over me,

his thin hands cupping the two blades
of my shoulders. Hot ice was what I felt –
a melting and stiffening, a strange tug
in my thighs, blood rushing everywhere.
He had to go home at last, and so did I.
But I stayed and swayed on the pier
to watch the wing-rowing pelicans pause
in mid-air before they released themselves
from their bodies' bows, and dove
into the amethyst waters below.

At Seventeen

One night we steered over the embankment
and into the glistening fields
blackened by the weight of dew and dark,
the Buick shrugging once before it
eased itself into unconsciousness,
and calmly we told ourselves that this time
we'd leave clothing and blankets behind;
so we strode out naked into the wilderness.

Shivering beneath a damp, triangular pine
that hung four stars like spiders
from its arms, we turned to one another
with frightened sighs, and kissed.
But what could the touch of lip on lip
do but make us feel smaller than the crickets
tuning their strings, or than the wind that
carried our voices off like balloons into the sky?

Twigs snapped under our weight, and moss
held us impressed into its green, spongy mass.
Something like a laugh broke above our heads:
an owl hooting at our awkwardness.
We knew then we needed to learn from the ferns
that clung to us, from the darkness that held us
hostage in its house, and from the earth which
gave us a bed and asked for nothing in return.

Clothes That Wear Me

1. DRESS

One day the voices of twenty women
singing a Gregorian chant caused a dress
to materialize out of the air.
It fit me perfectly, and even buttoned itself
in front, without my having to lift a finger.
When I went down the street in this dress
men fell to their knees, sparrows stopped
their small talk to follow me.
The zipper in the back sang Ave Maria,
and the pockets were lined with lilies.
Oh my dress full of ballads,
my dress that accepted me like a flask –
how could I lose you that night
I gambled with those young men
and their loaded dice?

2. WINTER CLOAK

I've taken the selfishness of men
and sewn a winter cloak out of it.
Its holes are the size of small towns
with storms hovering over them.
I can never iron out its wrinkles,
so I toss it into the furnace where,
naturally, it refuses to burn.
I'm stuck with wringing out its tears.

It's true, from chin to ankle I'm weak.
I can only say "no" on odd days;
I weep over the deaths of spiders,

those asterisks on the staircase.
But my mind, my sanitarium of a mind,
has the strength of three thousand
infantry men planting geraniums
in the desert. Such strength
recedes when I wear my angry coat,
my barren coat, my coat that
absorbs my life like a sponge.

3. FAVORITE THINGS

My favorite bra is bright blue.
One cup is larger than the other
so that my heart has room to expand.
This bra speaks now and then.
It abhors Neo-Expressionism,
black underwear, fluorescent lights.
Lately it's been encouraging me
to become a wetnurse to mankind.
My bra argues for divine love,
the milk of human kindness.
It's quickly falling out
of my favor.

My favorite shoe is shaped like a book.
When I put my right foot in it
I become a great, golden Buddha
pulling gently on my earlobes –
suddenly I can read the whole,
miraculous world in a glance.
When I put my left foot in it
I shrink down to a water beetle.

Then I scurry in-between the litter
of words, circumventing commas
and periods, and row through
the silences on each page.

4. VEILS

Far away my dead children
are putting on their veils.

First they press them with tiny irons,
and then they hold them up to the light.

Taking turns, the three infants tie
diaphanous veils around each other's heads.

When they wear their veils they see
everything that ever was or will be.

When they lift off their veils they cry.
For them, eternity is inexplicably sad.

As a mother of exiles, I never loved these children,
but I cried when my body turned them out.

Now they gather their flocks of stones,
as a chandelier of rain hangs over them.

Their veils are clouded with longing,
their faces were made to shine.

At Mudumalai

That day we arrived with the dust
of a thousand miles clamping our mouths shut,
we didn't care if the government cottage
had hot water, or mid-day tiffin, or lice.
We fell into mosquito-netted beds
and slept an even, unjoustled sleep.
We awoke cured, our bare arms
flung open to the fan's blades.
We sat on two heirlooms from the Raj,
stools made from an elephant's severed feet,
while a bearer named Ganesh brought tea.

On the third night the mahout arrived
with his well-mannered elephant
and her long-lashed calf.
In the moonlight the mother looked
like a dark house the baby leaned against.
At daybreak she knelt down before us,
her great trunk poised between
the flapping ears like a gentle cobra.

All day we swayed past deer tribes:
the lovely chital, the tiny mouse deer,
the stately gaurs. Once,
a boar burst out of the brush,
stopped, huffed in alarm, and left.
Red parakeets sprayed out of red flowers,
then followed a hill mynah's oration
as it teased its way into the distance.

Far behind us, Madras, with its secret trysts,
jumbled streets dizzy with despair,

clotted with goats, diesel smoke, rickshaws —
and even farther, the slow sleep
of your village, where the dry heat
drew scorpions out of the rafters, and
where local women lowered their eyes,
smiling, as they passed our doorway.

Now each rising every night
while the other slept, staggering
out under the cold weight of moonlight,
we watched the banyans shift
their hundred arms and legs, and saw
the stars wobble overhead. So,
in our separate sleep we dreamed
we floated tandem, hand-in-hand,
upon the Moyar River —
my hair splayed out in a corona,
your knees scraps of white paper —
as we drifted down the darkly-lit waters,
down to the plains of fire.

Commander-in-Chief Road

From the verandah looking down
to the road's straight arm – sunburnt,
hairless, but for a patch of dense green
near its wrist – here, every day
I watch sleek crows cross-stitch
the heavy cloth of monsoon skies.
The rumble of thunder, or of wooden wheels
carting laundry over Cooum River Bridge,
trembles in mid-air, then disappears.

Downstairs you sleep, child
to whom I'm both aunt and stranger,
the two of us reborn into new skins.
Your life swells the house with awe.

Now, at noon, everyone lies down.
But I look out upon the ceremonies
of the street, a goat munching a tire,
cow dung garlanded by butterflies,
and I wonder about the small weight
of your being, how each of us
carries it on a different arm.

Now, as you dream your infant dreams,
far across the Egmore rooftops
boys sail their paper kites, and banners
of dancing saris flap on the lines.
And beyond the road's gesture of hope,
with its flexed finger pointing the way

out into the world, is the country
we left behind, with its one great goddess
lifting her torch over the harbor.

I hear how she calls to each of us,
not just to the homeless, the bedraggled
orphans abandoned by wars, poverty.
What she says is what I would say
to you, Joshua, on your fifth day of life —
extend your clenched palms, reach beyond
your body: may a million blessings
fill your bowl like grains of rice.

Madras Lament

All night the nightwatchman pounds his stick
against the rust-red dirt of our road.
And curled against the papaya's display,
a pi-dog snores, half her golden fur gone
from asofoetida or mange. Off in the distance
peacocks wail, clouds rearrange themselves
in a flotilla of sails whitening the horizon.

I am up, as usual, at this hour, filling
my mind with the fan's arithmetic, the sighs
issuing from other rooms, the busy quiet.
Somewhere, beyond Egmore District, the sound
of a night train travels the darkness;
and from the direction of Mount Road, I hear
a monkey's chatter, the angry retort of a crow.

I've spent a year of wakefulness in this bed,
awaiting some midnight revelation.
June's monsoon has come and gone, leaving
behind a million silver holes in the road.
Life's balanced between known and unknown,
between the thwocks of a watchman's stick
and the dusty clatter of far-off hooves.

I slip out of the mosquito netting again
to pad across the cool marble to the balcony.
A terrible beauty shines from the stars,
as if the lies of time regild their petals.
I think it's loss that's wrung me out:
my lover an ocean beyond bullock carts,
night-blooming jasmine, and the starving

asleep in their rags, their palms frozen
open like cups, their closed faces aglow,
their shadows pooled into ochre stains.
But I'm wrong: it's the approaching light,
hastening like another storm toward the city,
that pierces me to this surrender,
that makes me cry out for such splendor.

Contusion

The fraction of a second it took
to sever the thin white cord, that
vessel that carries off your seed,
I saw the doctor's hands perform
their legerdemain under the spot-
light, and you groggy as a sailor,
shipwrecked, cast ashore, sat up
to see the blue testis exposed,
your thighs trembling so wildly:
the body's spasm of despair.

He was too nervous for comfort,
the doctor whose son committed
suicide by laying himself down
on steel ties, a sacrifice to
the gods of locomotion; though
why he sweated while you poked
through your shroud of seconal
has always made me doubt him,
as if he needed to be perfect
to legitimize my brusque calm.

Though eight years have passed,
and our daughters have doubled
themselves in our delight,
that scene reappears so solidly
it seems an intaglio of memory;
and I see again and again your
inconsolable loss, so subtly
hidden by your pride, how your
jaw grew tight as a current
of light in you switched off.

For Naomi

Last night you sleepwalked down the stairs,
dressed in your nakedness as a candle is
in its own glow. Perhaps you answered the sound
of wind dragging its chains through the trees,
or merely caught the scent of moon.
Whatever it was, you surprised me awake:
for your body, that fierce, white flame,
that early lily, lit up the stairwell.
I thought, where did my child go?

I thought of the rings of Jupiter, confusion
of lights, the bands of love around your life.
I thought of Grandma Rose, whose nakedness
startled me as a child into terror,
to think one so brittle could still allure.

And I wanted to cover your small shoulders
with the armor of my body, or with
an awkwardness people turn away from
calmly, as from the ordinary.
I wanted to dream you into a sanctuary
where no one could enter but the pure of heart.
I took your hand and led you up the stairs,
though even in that double darkness,
your body was already finding its way.

Anniversary Sonnet

Stopping to rest, we washed our hands
in the river, do you remember?
What are those dark fish, you asked.
What happens to them will happen to us.

I thought, It is simple to be a man,
simple to be a woman if we love
what is brief, what is given to us,
and clear the gloom with it.

We stood up, walked back to the world.
The sunset deepened the house's hush.
What marvelous lives we live, you said,
without saying anything at all.

Our children, sunlight on the wall.
On our tongues, the past, a drop of gold.

The White Cockroach

When my grandfather arrived from South Africa,
a sixteen year old wunderkind, to found
a small trousers factory in San Francisco,
he'd dreams every greenhorn had, of owning
a house on Nob Hill, of tying a silk jabot
over a freshly starched collar.

Back in Hull, before Johannesburg, he'd heard
Teddy Roosevelt played polo on the White House lawn,
and thought he could see himself amidst the pop
of flashbulbs and the clink of crystal glasses.
He married a Jewish debutante from Kansas,
and waited wisely for his luck to swell.

And one day, after the Chinese workers
had trudged out into the perpetual fog, and
Samuel had locked his factory doors the way
a banker locks his vault, he found a white cockroach
scuttling across his great mahogany rolltop desk.
Indeed, he'd seen marvels in his day:

diamonds the size of baby fists, and a pair
of Siamese twins named Tweedle Dee and Dum, even,
when he was ten, the Loch Ness monster raising
its pointed head out of the dawn-dark waters.
But this insect seemed, if anything, an omen,
a propitious charm that promised riches.

Secretly my grandfather confined his cockroach
to a bamboo cricket cage, and fed it daily
doses of buttered toast and homemade jam.
It grew more translucent in his desk drawer,

and voiced a curious clicking whenever it rained.
Sleek its feelers, sleek its wings folded up

like tiny kid gloves along its back; he named it
Caruso, and would stroke its thorax while it sang.
Meanwhile he grew rich, in a modest way, but always
uneasy that at any moment his luck could turn,
as the cream in his coffee sometimes did, go sour.
And, meanwhile, the cockroach had made a nest

from tufts of lint and stray threads, and laid
a pouch of pearly eggs that quickly hatched
into a swarm of rice-sized cockroaches – all
hungry and hardy as Samuel once had been.
But they unnerved him, reminding him of teeth
he'd lost as a child, of the white ashes

from his sister's death that blew back in his face
after he'd tossed them in the Bay from a rented boat.
Within a week his factory burned down, his wife
Rose got diabetes, and the huge white roach died.
Smoke, ashes, the smell of sodden cotton trousers.
Nothing left of value but an insurance check.

I look out from his Nob Hill rooms, one day after
his death and departure from the world, and think
about the diary in my lap that speaks of nothing
else but this albino mascot, strange bug of his.
Did he love his sons, his daughter – I think not
as much as he loved what lived beyond their grasp:

some dream of a pure wealth, a kind of white power
that would raise him above his loneliness and grief.
In these pages I hear Samuel wail and weep.
I turn his grim photograph to the window's light,
so he can look out over the blue, distant water
that cares neither for my words nor his quiet.

Theme and Variations

What is dark and oblique in a face –
eclipses under the eyes, the throat's blackness
pushing against the teeth, pupils welling up
with midnight, cobwebs and crow's feet
penned deftly with thin ink, a sunken sadness
in the cheeks, brow – such things teach us
how life seeps in, millimeter by millimeter,
into our tender disquietude of places.
Just as our breath heaves us in and out of ourselves,
just as the good muscles stretch and contract,
as the heart storms and calms itself perpetually,
so the face wears both sides, day and night,
on its skin, becomes both prison and garden.

My face nears forty now
and begins to play with new shadows.
They must crop up from beneath the light,
strange blooms that thrive blindly.
Now I approach the mirror as a confidante,
with the deliberation of a Solomon gone dim,
with the fecund look of a stagnant pond,
with an air that hangs with the weight of loss,
lifeless as a smudge of oil on parchment.
And when I question it, my mirror answers me:
Yes, childhood is just a dream your body devised.
Or, *You are a stone, a canvas, a wild
and abandoned place without walls.*

Days of Awe

"God can only be present in creation
in the form of absence." – SIMONE WEIL

Dancing cheek to cheek, your parents once
must have tango-stepped the twenties, drunk

on sorrel wine, tipsy with adolescent passion.
In Panama, where rhododendrons tripped the sun,

and army ants in silent parade undressed slain
lizards down to the bone, you sold your name

for a harlot's license when you were seventeen.
You knew enough by then: death of a beloved friend –

your despair a catacomb, dark as a monsoon cloud.
Perhaps you could only paint your way out;

perhaps those early sketches, as fluid as wind
over water, were a kind of shadow talk from within.

Back in Boston, and years beyond there to here,
you learned to live with absence, could stare

it down, pare it into whirling moths of light
that rise from your one-eyed, wooden palette

to the canvas, fiercely as filings to a magnet. Art!
Mother, what starry configuration of the heart,

what voluptuous dreams gathered into a hymn,
what delirious soul dances beneath your skin?

No gesture in the universe is ever lost:
a cricket singing with its wings, a host

of petals spinning, fleet clouds that touch
the mirror of the moon's face to polish.

Marriage, that great synthesizer, was, I'm sure,
a kind of gesture, wasn't it? To abide there

at its center, as at the center of being, meant
postponing the separating of waters, it meant

keeping part of yourself under cover, like those
crickets cranking out songs from severed roses:

marriage is a strange sleep that tows the dreamer,
that reinvents the clock. It accelerates art.

And children, those phantom limbs hollowed for love,
how we pleased you, how we seized like a glove

your tenderness, brief flesh of your flesh,
how we punished you for it with our arrogance.

Forty years adrift, you expected the cactus
to grow wings, the moon to scour its rust —

and they have, they have! Not a single gesture
lost, only a perfecting of rapture.

The click and shiver of memory haunt me.
What is printed inside the roots of a tree

remains a mystery to me, as does the shape
of death astride its white stag, or the lake

under which our ancestors sleep stacked
like spoons. I look at your paintings backed

against the walls and feel my heart repair itself.
Your every touch is lyric, your embrace felt

even by the wilted purple zinnias in the room.
At night I watch your colors step from their two-

dimensional tombs to raise the rooftop.
Don't let fame's twisted face taunt you now,

nor the concatenation of years chain you to the past:
your genius waltzes alone in the cathedral's vast

worship; alone, completely alone, undaunted.
Today the sun blooms like a poppy, and the taut grid

called heaven is awash with brilliant stars.
Sixty leave-takings, sixty greetings, sixty years!

Mother, listen: your paintings speak to us
about how absence, itself, is a wondrous house.

11

In the Shtetl

Was it astonishment or fear or both
that guided men into the iron bars of despair
one night, and kept them locked up tight
and holding hands under their long sleeves?
To comfort them the rabbi said:
Even before the world existed, the Torah
existed, having been written
with black fire on white fire;
it lay on the lap of God.

But the men could hear horses' hooves
like cumulative thunder getting nearer.
And the boastful thud of cannonballs
recalled their fathers' warnings:
Among our pages full of smoke and blood,
you must cling to the edge of the story.

It seemed that all around them
the world waltzed in a flaming skirt,
and that the exiled souls of the dead
surrounded them with moans.
A conference of crows on the farthest horizon,
the phantom of a dome in Bucharest,
deadened water in a silver bowl:
all signs, impurities.

Let the house be filled from the ground
to the roof in prayers, what good was piety?
Evil weakened the strong; the left foot
and right foot wore the same stocking.
Who could prepare for the Days of Awe,
the Day of Atonement in this fever of silence?

Then one who had never spoken arose.
And when he began to sing,
his voice dark and robust as a Guarneri's,
the men saw his small soul flare
beneath his body's lantern, like light
beneath parchment. *Listen! Listen!*
Within his song the thunder subsides,
the moon wings into the windowframe,
they whispered. At last,

his music lulled the world, so in that calm
they heard, not from the Kingdom of Mysteries,
but from the kitchen, the clear voice
of the rabbi's daughter calling,
calling them in to dinner.

Vermeer's Women

How absent-mindedly they hold the light
that bathes them, the light chilled
against the air before it warms to their skins,
before it enters their calm bodies and
tenderly occupies their faces.
And poised in their faces a completeness
of the self, a sturdy radiance.
How is it the world can be so utterly forgotten
that all the hubbub of horses, vendors,
servant banter, water wheels, and roosters
fades into the stillness of a gesture?
The impasto of colors thickens them,
the damp Delft weather rubs their cheeks
with a soft vermeil rag, and even the details
of their lives – maps, loaves of bread, dogs –
grow lustrous as if such things
gain substance only in the presence
of such women. Spellbound, the world recedes.
And they, with their beauty lost
to themselves by the dailiness of their lives,
pause between centuries,
and by pausing, blaze momentarily
and always.

Icarus in the Twentieth Century

Sometimes it comes to him when he's awake,
and the dream of falling off the edge
of the world tilts him forward slightly.
Even his father, who is both a lure
and a warning, is bent so far down
to the ground that the earth descends
like stairs before him.

So he steadies himself and when he feels
himself falling he ties stones to his shoes.
His children, wide-eyed, have caught him
with white knuckles clutching the armchair
or crawling on the rug, as if hunting
for a lost pin. They too begin to tilt,
to cling to furniture.

Tired of pushing picture frames askew,
and of hooking him to lamp standards
at the tops of hills, his wife buys him
books on gravity, astronomy, dream analysis.
But she knows eventually he'll fall from her,
and tells him he must learn to love what
slips away each year.

Driven down like a stake into despair,
he travels by boat to Tierra del Fuego, then
to Cape Horn where, doubled-over and shivering,
he opens his arms as he leaps off a cliff.
But instead of being hurtled down,
he's lifted up out of his heavy shoes
like a paper airplane,

the world curving away beneath his feet
as he sails through storm clouds, flocks
of cormorants, roving shoals of flying fish.
The air rushes past his ears like applause.
When he returns he finds his father collecting
feathers, his wife vertical, his children's gaze
afixed to the horizon.

King Midas's Daughter

She retires to the tower, her only haven
away from the artless glare of gold.
Weighted down with plums and a melon
not yet hardened by her father's hold,
she mounts the stone stairs, her steps fierce,
her long red hair uncoiling from its spiral.
From the window the far waves break in tiers;
he will not touch them, he is too fearful
to leave his glowing world, his golden throne.
Against the curved blade of the horizon,
she sees a ship with fluttering sails blown
dangerously close to the harbor: *Don't come,*
she silently commands it, and it goes.

She is like a plant calling for water.
She is like a fist pounding a pillow.
She's forgotten the taste of her own laughter,
and the sound of a mockingbird in the willow.
She sees him below in a garden among statues
that are grotesque, familiar, golden.
And he's calling up to her now: *Come choose
a flower, any flower!* And his foolish exuberance
makes her jump from her chair and rush to him,
wanting to shake this curse from his shoulders,
wanting to hug his thinning body, unloosen
its cold grief, its sorrow of greed, however
he scolds her, or dazzles her into silence.

The Doves of Pliny

When you spat out wild grape seeds,
your tongue a small windmill,
I thought of stars spewed out like darts,
and afixed to the tail of the Milky Way.

And when you bit off the ends of words,
one hand dangling from the bath,
the other carving swans from the air,
I thought your silences as lovely as songs.

Now that smoke and ash have cleared,
I've set a bowl of clear water on a balustrade.
Your two doves come to drink, their heads
casting green shadows that cross like daggers.

How can I forget all you taught me?
I have journeyed to the moon and back,
to the stone reefs at sea's bottom, even
into the human heart, astride your pages.

I've met men with backward-turned toes,
the Mouthless Men who live on beauty alone,
on the merest fragrance of peony and fig,
and those Umbrella Feet, with their soft skin.

All those monstrosities, winged snakes,
single-eyed, spout-horned beasts abound
despite the stone eye of Aristotle,
which always stared beyond amazement.

Uncle, uncle, they've carried your body away,
though you looked asleep rather than dead –

Why wouldn't you rush to the boat with me
instead of standing, a pillow pressed to your lips,

the sulphuric fumes clouding your thoughts,
the blackness engulfing you like ink a fish?
As I ran I saw your slaves pulling you upright
amidst the shrieking crowds, but you fell again.

Was it your scorn for immortality, that hag
with wine skins for breasts, that kept you
talking long after your guests had fled?
Or was it some stubborn loyalty to science?

The doves bob their pretty heads, their wings
fold behind them like fans, their eyes
are bewildered by your unlikely silence.
Their every note lights a torch in my throat.

Now Catullus hides away in his Sirmio villa,
his purse of cobwebs collecting tears.
All Verona wails. Vesuvius still smoulders.
Uncle, hear the sadness in the wheels.

The Elevator

Darling, you undress me
every morning with your rough eyes
as we ascend the elevator
to the ninth floor of this building:
do you expect me to be surprised
when we jerk to a halt, and the door
causes you to press your shoulder
against my sweatered breast?
Your breath escapes as slowly then
as a word in French, and a tremor
hovers on your lips as you sweat.

Though I'm used to being open
with men – I've bedded too many
to count – I like this pantomime,
this longing at nine and at five,
that we carry on up and down, honey.
Yet you look so raw, young, leonine.
Me, I'm thirty-nine, divorced, twice.
Still, we're all greedy for love;
all of us clumsy, cocked for sex.
We're almost there: the electric jolt,
the bumping grind, the sudden rush
of air, the stammer of feet, legs,
and then, strangers again, we're out.

The Gardener

Small petitioners, the bees revisit
the custard blossoms to plea for pollen,
and the darning needles stretch their wings,
then stitch two lines across a puddle.

Mr. Bombay slams his garden boots against
the steps to loosen last spring's mud,
then scratches his neck, trying to decide
shall it be radishes or not this year.

Near the compost, turtledoves bob heads
as they hunt for fallen berries, sow bugs.
Gnats careen against themselves, while
a dandified robin eyes the white cat.

Mr. Bombay finds himself here, euphoric
amidst the odors of cow manure, fish emulsion.
Already he can smell the greening of peas,
the jubilant tomatoes ripening so redly;

he can taste the quick thrill of chilies,
the complex sweetness of figs and apricots.
Leaning against his spade's pole, he finds
among the imaged bounty through which

he drifts, a communion with the soil, so
does his own life seem to ripen and decay,

enriched by its own pain, wetted by tears.
Quickly he drops to his knees in the dirt,

and nuzzles his face in the decay-sweet lap.
Here is where he will sink, after the final
harvest: his body a dark, radiant room,
his memory, a root breaking ground.

The Surreal Man

He has a coconut head, brown and bewildered.
Two Dead Sea scrolls for ears,
he hears the rustle of ancient lips,
the clatter of silver fins beneath the water.
With peppercorn eyes, he often mistakes
winter's thin works for a summer exuberance.
But his mouth is exact as a zero,
because it is only a mouth in theory.
In practice, it's a cry the size of a thumbtack.

How pure his thoughts, how sweet and white.
The three dark spots on his crown see
only the undersides of birds and clouds,
the foreshadowing of weather.
His shoulders are two toupees,
lost from a brigadier general's middle age.
His chest is a cardboard box filled
with bicycle parts, and there's
an accordian for his heart
that squeaks when squeezed, and sometimes
stops when women press its red keys down.

Telephone poles for arms and legs,
he's a bit stiff-jointed, and the scent
of tar and circuits permeates his skin.
But what hands! Lilies for palms, a supply
of matchsticks for fingers – he can both
singe and pollinate his friends and lovers.
It's true: his penis is a small cannon
stuffed with grapeshot, his balls red onions.
For his knees, two large postage stamps
from China commemorating the giant panda.

And his feet, those magnificent feet!
Made of human flesh, they're as strong
and stubborn as landlords.
Only these staunch feet keep him from taking
off like a rocket into the stratosphere.
When he dies, these feet, alone, will survive.
Disembodied, they'll walk the earth,
trailing the empty sack
of his shadow behind them.

The Rabbi's Trousers, Circa 1900

Fridays find him bent over the cloth of prophets.
Dybbuks gloat from the mantel, green-eyed,
and their crooked horns golden in the glass.

It's hot here, but downstairs hotter
where wide women work their knuckles
into dough, spitting in an iron stove.

Covered with embroidered letters, Moses
paces the old world two floors above
Brooklyn's stony clatter, bony voices.
His black silk trousers rustle on a chair.
They whisper "adulterer, infidel,"
these pants that form the center
of a summer storm, the devil's leggings
which will walk him through a maze of alleys
sour with filth and longing.

Downstairs an iron skates across
a board and two children, bearing
his name, squabble for matzoh.

Oh Sophia, Sophia
he calls over the rooftops
of corrugated copper, *Sophia*
dimpling the clouds with stitches
of rain, *Sophia* draped
in the vines of heaven,
he calls her name as she rises
from the baths, as she shakes
rosewater over her clean breasts.

Yes, he will be polite to God and clasp
his ceramic hands to his heart,
and he will pray himself into wax
like a candle burning at both ends.

Slowly he unwraps his shawls, puts down again
the sacred, floret scroll, and pulls on the pants —
his legs plunging deep into the black waters —
pulls them on over his tassel-knotted robes.

The Palmist

In a doorway she holds the wrist
of the night in one hand,
and the palm of some sailor
in the other.
She says, Ah yes,
there's sadness here
in the Strait of Magellan,
or, I see great joy residing
in the Mound of Venus,
joy huge as a copper pot.

Each day fills with speechless signs,
but she ignores them.
She embeds herself like a nail
in her own life.
Men twirl their moustaches
to see her rose of a mouth,
her delicate eyebrows.
But her thoughts are on
their hands, the snowy tongues
of flesh, crosshatchings of veins.
She sees their ships drowning,
their many wives
wrapped in shawls of frost.

One day she marries an admiral
who wears striped pants.
His smile's an anchor.
Sundays on the way to the park,
they hold hands,

their lives webbed together.
Sitting sole to sole
in the tall grass,
their laughter floats
between them like a stone meadow
over which their sorrows break.

Nude Mice

In the night laboratory they take on a glow.
Little electric bulbs, they move about
in greys and pinks and blacks.
Their ugliness is extreme, beautiful.

Unlike Frankenstein's pets,
they are without guile.
And better yet, they lack the will
to resist transformation:

we'll graft a lizard's scaly belly on one,
and soon he'll be doing push-ups
with the iguanas;

we'll sew a bird's tummy on another
and lo and behold, he'll sprout feathers!

Tonight we're hoping for a miracle
of sorts: we're attaching the platelets
from a dragon's back onto the spine
of our bravest mouse.
We hope such efforts will result
in a renewed interest in fairy tales.

Tomorrow night we graft the curl
of a pig's tail, a dragonfly's wings,
a rattlesnake's rattle, a bear's growl
to four different specimens.

Theoretically we're torn between
the pragmatic and the metaphysical.
And ever since we dreamed
them into the world,
we've been shivering.

The Pharaohs

They lie quietly within their deaths.
Gone the singing flesh, fever

of light, the sands of eternal grief.
Their skins become papyrus upon which

no one writes, and their arms cross
over the emptiness in their hearts.

Stray hairs of evening slip through
the sarcophagus lids in needles

that stitch the past to a single moment,
joining the end of the world

to its beginning. A buzz of hunger
wanders the corridors to other rooms.

One by one, the pharaohs sit up to listen
closely to the vaulted darkness.

Down the well of a nostril, the fly
burrows its pearl-shaped verses.

Down the Nile, ships with lanterns break
into hieroglyphs the moonlit waters.

The Abandoned Church

Who knew how long it had languished,
its windows open to each winter's migration
of wasp and black widow, and its huge door
long since closed to the hungry in spirit.

Vagrants had swarmed there once, lit fires
in the center of the basilica, leaving
the floor charred and cluttered with jars
and votive candles filled with cinders.

High up, the domed apse spilled the colors
some artist sieved from heaven: untroubled
blues chastening the misplaced cornices,
a rose corolla opening its fiery petals,

and the comet-like stars shooting themselves
across the ceiling in silver and gold gilt.
All the church's glory had been summoned
to float above the heads of the faithful.

But elsewhere was a barrenness too apparent
to be dismissed or forgotten; the walls
peeling, the pews removed, even the altar
soiled by rain, disuse, a fall from grace.

Only a madonna remained to flower there
in the dusky nave draped with cobwebs.
Her head tilted to one side, her smile
a half smile, half frown, her eyes averted:

she presided over the ruined church,
her long green gown frozen to her skin,
her slender hands rubbed brown by worry,
by the touch of a thousand fingertips

or more, and her feet clad, like a child's,
in cloth slippers. Only her eyes were still,
unapproachable in their intense drilling
of the air, lost in the absence of prayer.

Gallows

Under the shadow's claw
where red petals riot with moonlight,
the charwoman remembers the colonel,
his kind indifference, his black boots
falling over themselves beneath the bed.

Another colonel arrives tomorrow,
but she will not attend the welcome
when the mayor offers up his daughter
to be kissed by bristling whiskers,
and makes a speech about duty, honor.

One man's death makes way for the golden
glory of another. And life goes on.
The woman watches the frayed rope swing,
knowing that in time another head
will offer its pendulum to history.

And who now bothers to count
the moonlit daggers piercing the planks,
or to tally up the silver coins she
collected at dawn in naked shame?
She'll go to church, pray for them all.

III

Angle of Repose

Sometimes, when the sky leans back
to lower itself into the hammocked hills,
and when acacia trees lay out their shadows
across the green bay, we put down
our pens to pause over
the faint-hearted light sweeping
a rooftop, swerving past waving branches
as it settles to the ground.

Only at such times do we hear lost spirits
whistling in the stale weeds
like reckless boys we once knew, or the zig-
zagging call of whippoorwills cutting
through the always distant fields
where bright blue cornflowers grow,
impervious to these sounds.

Being half-submerged
in time, when we pause in this way
we are lifted to the day's surface,
and we see how so few
of our ripples ever reach shore
without returning.
At this angle, we know what a life is.
It is an eye for the light
that lengthens as it drops,
and an ear for the rustle of movement
beyond the stillness of the heart.

Encounter

Suddenly, from the tip of a tall yucca,
a hummingbird rises, then flies to me,
its beak parted, its wings fanning my face.

It orbits my head once, twice, then pauses
as we drink each other in, the bird's body
barely aquiver, its wings beating the air.

I hold my breath, it holds its eye to mine,
then dips its head to look over my green dress,
the web of my hair, my smooth, bare feet.

It's plain that one of us is a mirage
that the other has imagined into being.
Or that we're both having the same dream.

I'm caught up by the metallic sheen and whirl:
poise and purpose sculpted into sheer joy.
A cheep, and the hummingbird disappears.

The Sadness of Rivers

The sadness of rivers is their aimlessness.
Though the edge of the world invites them,
they refuse to go beyond themselves.
Even the wolves of destiny can't persuade them
to forsake the lyric poem for the epic.

The contentment of trees is their protocol;
always bowing good-day, waving good-bye,
they make a ceremony out of greening.
They even put up with the coal-hearted crow,
with ruptured kites, and an armor of snow.

The bitterness of mountains is a solid fire,
banked and fueled by an envy of clouds.
With hearts of granite, mountains are unmoved
by the sight of swans reshaping the skies,
by the slow deaths of free-wheeling stars.

The joy of roses is a breaking of silence;
their fragrance a translation of light.
Their marvelous bodies spell out desire
in the coldest years of exile, when hunger
sings in the ice and despair licks itself.

The wisdom of oceans is a holy invention.
Though waves love to confess their passions
to unlistening shores, the ancient scrolls

of spindrift retain their pearly secrets,
the waters of oblivion seal their doors.

The gratitude of stones is wide as the world.
Their shadows are heirlooms the day hoards,
along with the blessings of pebbles.
Stones know the words under our tongues
are their children: mutable, jagged, bold.

The Inheritance

Three men traveled alongside this road
one night, half-hidden by a row of hedges,
half-drunk and ready to battle demons.
They were numb to the cold, numb to the kiss
the pale moon placed on their necks.
Their fists were clenched, and the snow deep.
They fought over a bet or a girl or a plow,
and one man was killed.

One man turned west, and one turned east.
The dead man spread out his life in red
on a sheet of snow, and a single bird wept.
Why didn't the world for just one moment
stop, why didn't all creation halt?
Those who love him join him on this step
into darkness, of which he owns a portion.
This stillness is his breath, his wisdom.

The Years

Green apples hang like worlds
above the perpetuating yard,
as clouds dismantle this slow season
and the next, and even the classic
stand of oaks is finally gnarled

by all the elements of change –
by windswipe and fitful sun, by dust
that doesn't rest for any cause, and
by the rain that circles everything,
that orchestrates decay's exchange.

If only I could eclipse the fall
of all the lives I love; if I
could halt the wheel that grinds
us down, one by one, into the ground,
I'd let the seasons slow and stall.

And if I thought stalling could be bought,
I'd sell my breath in bundles, my heart
in drumbeats by the fraction of the ounce.
But such dreaming's merely helplessness
that stands in front of death, agog.

The years get blurred in nameless ways.
We age: our bodies slacken, our voices
climb their fearful ladders; we sway.
One day we loosen our clutch upon the bough
and let the years carry us away.

Rothko's Black

The painting glows savagely,
calmly, and the world floats off
in a square, flat discus,
then reappears as a thunderstorm
viewed from a canvas window.

Such darkness calls to us
from beyond the body's ocean;
it calls to us from the other side
of love, where we ghost through
looking glass faces.

For here's a blackness of sound
deep as a baritone's silence,
and tuned to the key of Self.
We're black boats now,
black sails, oars.

We begin to row back
and forth from lighthouse
to lighthouse.

Death's Earned No Diplomas

Death's earned no diplomas,
and needs no formal education.
He comes and lays a thumb upon your lips,
says "Open wide." No calling card.
You turn your face away, but there
he is again, straddling you in bed, a knee
on either side of your ribcage.
He works his way into your mouth,
spreads your teeth you try
to clench, and slips right in.
And then he's there to stay, pulls down
the shades over your eyes, cuts off
the lines that bind you to the world,
takes you hostage.
And when, years later, he finally
goes away, you're an empty house with all
its lop-sided windows broken, all
its doors flung open,
and its furnace still smoking.

Dream Babies

Double-chinned or fine fingered,
webtoed, chagrined malingerers,
despoilers of diapers, night
balkers, day squawkers:
a bounty of babies visits me.
They coo like miniature muses,
their tongues wet, petulant fuses;
they snap at my dry nipples,
those poor doorbells, my dead eyes
rising to their open mouths
like anxious buttons.
How my uterus tightens now,
shrinks to a triangular diamond;
how my cervix snickers.
Why do they come nightly,
this army of whimperers,
this hungry parade, beating
their rattles against my ribcage,
tearing off their bibs?
Take us, take us, they beg,
butter our chins with love,
this-little-piggy our fingers.
This can't go on much longer.
The honeycombs are overfilled
with larvae, the bees drag
their pollen-powdered legs
over the garden, the anthills
swarm with soldiers, the dead
gather in the darkroom.

Survival

I keep the scorpion, *Vejovis spinigerus,*
in a Mason jar filled with delicate corpses.
The carpenter ant has curled dryly into itself;
the white fairy moth is poised in death —
a tiny airplane that nose-dived, collapsed;
even the long-necked Raphidia lapsed
into motionlessness, stung to the quick.
This scorpion earns respect for keeping a wick
of breath lit, despite my cold, antagonistic eye.
But what of all these other creatures high
and low in jars, boxes, aquariums, cages?
Two frogs in two months have, in stages,
grown depressed and starved themselves to death.
And two infant deer mice, with huge heads,
refuse to suckle on the milk-doused Q-tip
I offer them; they, too, have begun to slip.
In every cranny and nook hosts of dying wings,
while the scorpion crooks his ready sting.
Only he and the hot-blooded hamster thrive;
the one feasting like a saint on sacrifice,
the other frantically spinning out the nights,
something electric keeping her alive.

In the Valley of Ether

I have drifted a short distance from myself.
Severed roses walk on water in the bowl,
the candle talks in tongues along the wall.

Pirate of venture, I steal away from my ship,
from its spinal mast, its grumbling hull,
its crow's nest snagged in the clouds.

My body, like an April citadel, or winter
isle of easy breezes, my body calls me back.
I will not go. I like the way I live now

for pauses between beats, with a metronome's
sweet expectation, or a divining rod's pull;
I know when I return to collect the dues

of the living, the daily rent of my yearning,
what is here right now will elude me.
I must finish what I begin, and welcome

the unknown, whether it rises as starlight
from the mouths of the dead, or whether it
sinks with the body into silent burning.

Tale Before the End of the World

We never had any doubt the world would end.
The message wavered over the air waves
in a bodiless echo. Sam packed the car
with peaches, wine, some macadamias we'd saved.
No need for a map of the mundane, or of the stars
that hid themselves in shame for us.
The children watched our faces closely,
hugging their dolls to their breasts.

Up we wound, higher and higher into ponderosas
clinging to the rain-scrubbed mountains.
A hawk swirled and floated over the road,
oblivious to the early chill, the emptiness
broadcast from the city's heart below.
Who would have thought such a world
could end, suddenly, like a dream?
We turned away from the thought.

Sorrow rose from the bark, from a string
of ants laboring under their tiny loads.
Sorrow balanced on a branch and sang
its sparrow song, and wrung its squirrel hands.
Sorrow opened and closed the breeze's lips,
sorrow seethed in sap, in leaf-vein, in blood.
The sorrow caught the fingertips of Anne,
our child, pulling her up from the ground.

I won't let the world die, she cried out
as the sorrow multiplied her soul and she
swelled until she loomed huge as a thunderhead –
her hands churning their windmills,

her eyes beaming their floodlights in farewell.
A human tornado, a magnet, she drew out
the poison from the world's silos,
from the minds and mouths of terror.

And that's how she saved the world.
We repacked the car and drove home,
though Anne never returned to us at all.
I spoon out the darkness and the light
at dinner time, and later touch my son
unborn beneath my skin, and hold my husband
in his death-tormented sleep. I lie in bed,
stricken by the silence of the house.

The Future

An airplane cruises above the clouds.
A stiff silver goddess, its arms spread wide,
it hums like a madonna singing hallelujah.

The puddles fill with rainbows of grease;
the cattails by the stream are microphones
into which the bees softly speak.

In the desert dromedaries carry jars
of boiling water, pumpkins, erotic verses.
Where, then, is the oasis of the heart?

And where will I be in one hundred years?
Will I lay low in some neglected field,
or return to hear my voice cradled now

in another human body, or else eased
from the throat of a lizard or a horse?
I'll go down the same way I arose, saying:

Bless the storytellers and their fragile tongues,
bless the bee-keepers, organ grinders, the women
and men who dance with their breasts just touching.

Star-studded night with its circles of rain,
mysterious light, white torch of moonlight –
the city's abandoned, the children looking for maps.

Les Fleurs du Printemps

Looking slightly kitsch, the birds-
of-paradise stretch their long necks
over the flagstone step.
I prefer cymbidia, with their open
mouths and tiny tongues feathering the air.
If flowers could talk, these orchids
would lisp in French, unlike the roses
which, no doubt, have mastered Sanskrit.
There by the rusty faucet the stamens
of the calla lilies seem so
grotesquely yellow, yet the bees
drop-stitch into them now,
as if the jaundiced fingers beckoned.
High above the flat-thumbed jade,
a passion flower crowns the arbor slats
with splendid nonchalance.
Here is the martyr on the cross –
mute, painfully beautiful – its purple-
tipped filaments stab heavenward,
its t-hinged anthers splay out
beneath that single, bold altar:
the pollen-swollen stigma,
its shape a human heart.

The Poem at the End of the World

Is a dark, pregnant girl sweeping
her doorway every dawn who

empties a handful of ashes over
a fist of pollen cradled in soil,

and it's the star she lights with
a match, and the sign on the rim

of her mailbox that offers Raw Honey,
and the lamp under her body's blanket,

and it's the shovel that spirits decay
back to her ancestors, and the pen

in her hand, near her heart's page,
that unwrites itself out of sorrow,

out of poverty's claw – see now down
the road she wanders, spelling her shadow

on a rise of trees, blinking in
the eyes of headlights – the poem

at the end of the world claps with
one hand as she dances through thorns,

as her red hair singes the air,
with her burning shirt made of tears,

her defiant ribbons, with her missing
front tooth, her lisping hope –

O distant with child, O abandoned by
death, she dances barefoot

through the silent wilderness,
her belly's prow parting the dark.

Atomic Psalm

Last night the stars seemed not themselves,
for they sang such a lonely song
I heard all creation weep along.
And the moon seemed too molten hot –
it burned a hole right through the roof,
right through the sky, it burned
an empty place into the night.

And oh how the world rocked
like a cradle in the ether of the dark.
And how the children, lost in dreams,
awoke with a start, not out of fear
but from surprise. They blinked their eyes
in that starless night, that moonless night,
and cried, though no one heard.

God-Who-Is-Not, give us a lock
of your immortal hair, or give us stars
that we can reach and hang upon the bars
of our despair; give us back the rock
called moon, that still, white face
we write our lives upon. Give us back
our dark hope in its golden case.

PAGE 21

Mudumalai is a game preserve in Tamil Nadu, South India, located on the northeastern slopes of the Nilgiris mountain range. A tiffin is a tiered, cylindrical lunch pail, made of brass or stainless steel.

PAGE 23

For Joshua Mohandas Ambroson. Egmore is a residential district in Madras, South India.

PAGE 30

For Samuel Simon (1888–1964).

PAGE 34

For my mother, Baila Goldenthal, and written upon the occasion of her sixtieth birthday.

PAGE 45

Pliny the Elder (a.d. 23–79) was the Roman author of the celebrated *Natural History in Thirty-Seven Books,* a storehouse of information about ancient mathematics, physics, meteorology, astronomy, biology, botany, zoology, mineralogy, and art. As prefect of the Roman fleet at Misenum, Pliny the Elder was stationed only miles away from the great Vesuvian eruption on August 24, 79. The poem is based on an account of the circumstances of Pliny the Elder's death, as written by his nephew, Pliny the Younger.

PAGE 47

For Robert Coover, and patterned after a character in his marvelous story, "The Elevator."

PAGE 52

For my great-grandfather, Moses Goldenthal (1865–1935).

PAGE 56

For the Czech poet, Miroslav Holub. Nude mice are specially developed laboratory animals which accept skin grafts more readily than normal mice, and which Dr. Holub uses frequently in his immunology research.

PAGE 82

For Liz Rosenberg, whose ear is finely attuned to the music of the spheres.